WHOPPING GREAT BIG BONKERS JOKE BOOK

Other Joke Books from Puffin

**THE SILLIEST
JOKE BOOK EVER**

**THE SILLIEST SCHOOL
JOKE BOOK EVER**

**THE GREAT MONSTER
JOKE BOOK**

**PUFFIN'S BRILLIANTLY
BIG BUMPER JOKE BOOK**

THE WHOPPING GREAT BIG BONKERS JOKE BOOK

PUFFIN BOOKS

With thanks to the following contributors:
Amanda Li, Kay Woodward, Dave Bromage,
Rhodri Crooks, John Byrne and Jane Richardson

PUFFIN BOOKS

Published by the Penguin Group
Penguin Books Ltd, 80 Strand, London WC2R 0RL, England
Penguin Group (USA) Inc., 375 Hudson Street, New York, New York 10014, USA
Penguin Group (Canada), 90 Eglinton Avenue East, Suite 700, Toronto, Ontario, Canada M4P 2Y3
(a division of Pearson Penguin Canada Inc.)
Penguin Ireland, 25 St Stephen's Green, Dublin 2, Ireland (a division of Penguin Books Ltd)
Penguin Group (Australia), 250 Camberwell Road, Camberwell, Victoria 3124, Australia
(a division of Pearson Australia Group Pty Ltd)
Penguin Books India Pvt Ltd, 11 Community Centre, Panchsheel Park, New Delhi – 110 017, India
Penguin Group (NZ), 67 Apollo Drive, Rosedale, North Shore 0632, Auckland 1310, New Zealand
(a division of Pearson New Zealand Ltd)
Penguin Books (South Africa) (Pty) Ltd, 24 Sturdee Avenue, Rosebank, Johannesburg 2196, South Africa

Penguin Books Ltd, Registered Offices: 80 Strand, London WC2R 0RL, England

puffinbooks.com

Published 2007
009

Text copyright © Puffin Books, 2007
Illustrations copyright © Ian Cunliffe, 2007
All rights reserved

The moral right of the illustrator has been asserted

Set in Phoenix Chunky, Countryhouse and Vag Rounded
Made and printed in England by Clays Ltd, St Ives plc

British Library Cataloguing in Publication Data
A CIP catalogue record for this book is available from the British Library

ISBN: 978-0-141-32313-8

www.greenpenguin.co.uk

MIX
Paper from
responsible sources
FSC
www.fsc.org   FSC™ C018179

Penguin Books is committed to a sustainable
future for our business, our readers and our planet.
This book is made from Forest Stewardship
Council™ certified paper.

CONTENTS

INTRODUCTION

Whether you like knock-knocks
or just plain old groaners,
you're bound to find your favourite joke
in our biggest joke book EVER!

We've got jokes about anything and everything –
from shy elephants, nutty aliens, crazy monsters and barmy
families to gags about chickens, strange doctors and school
antics. In fact, we have so many fantastic jokes, we are
confident that this is the WHOPPINGEST and most BONKERS
of all joke books in the history of the world!

So, how do we know?

Well, each joke has been subject to rigorous scientific testing
(i.e. we told them to anyone we could find, including people
in the office, children on the street and even the postie).
The funniest ones are in this book!

We do hope you have as much fun reading
this book as we had putting it together.
So dive in and start chuckling!

The Puffin Team

ANIMAL QUACKERS

You'll be roaring with laughter in no time with these gags!

What did the cat say when he ran out of money?
'I'm paw.'

What do you call a greenfly with no arms, legs or wings?
A boyey.

What do lions say before they start hunting?
'Let us prey . . .'

What's orange and sounds like a parrot?
A carrot!

Why wouldn't the leopard take a bath?
He didn't want to get spotlessly clean.

3

How does an elephant carry its things when it goes on holiday?
In its trunk.

What animal goes 'Oooo'?
A cow without lips.

Why did Tigger look down the toilet?
To find Pooh.

What do bees chew?
Bumble gum.

What animal is like a yogurt?
A moose.

What did the skunk say when the wind changed direction?
'It's all coming back to me now!'

Why did the girl have a pile of dirt on her shoulder?
Because she had a mole on her cheek!

Two monkeys were getting in a bath.
One monkey said, 'Oo, oo, oo, aah, aah, aah.'
The other monkey said, 'Well, put some cold in, then.'

What do you call a girl with a frog on her head?
Lily.

Why does a flamingo lift up one leg?
Because if it lifted up both legs it would fall over!

What happens when a frog breaks down?
It gets toad away.

What did the sheep say to his girlfriend?
'I love ewe!'

What do you do if you come face to face with an adder?
Subtract it!

Why don't pigs eat bacon?
Do you know a pig that can cook?

Why did the referee book the two chickens at the football match?
Because they fowled each other.

What type of chocolate
do lambs like best?
A big baaaaa.

Cow 1: 'Are you worried about
mad cow disease?'
Cow 2: 'No.'
Cow 1: 'Why not?'
Cow 2: 'Because I'm a mouse!'

What do bees do if they want
to get public transport?
They wait at the buzz stop!

What type of dog can you eat?
A hot dog.

Lovebird 1: 'Say something sweet to me.'
Lovebird 2: 'Marshmallow, chocolate, fudge, cake . . .'

What do you call a sheep with a machine gun?
Lambo.

Where do ducks keep their money?
In a river bank.

What is the definition of a snail?
A slug with a crash helmet.

What's worse than finding a maggot in your apple?
Finding half a maggot.

How do toads greet one another?
'Warts up!'

Newsflash

Animals are smarter than people!
A university has just carried out an
important study. Eight greyhounds
were brought together to race, and
10,000 people turned up to watch.
Shortly after, eight humans raced
each other, and not one animal
turned up to see it.

What do you call a donkey
with three legs?
A wonkey.

What sound to hedgehogs make when they kiss?
Ouch!

Why do bears have fur coats?
Because they can't get plastic macs in their size!

What do baby apes sleep in?
Apri-cots.

Did you hear about the flea who won the lottery?
He bought a dog in Spain.

Horse 1: 'Do you always eat hay?'
Horse 2: 'Well, I don't when I'm asleep!'

What do you get if you sit under a cow?
A pat on the head!

What's the definition of a slug?
A snail with a housing problem!

Why is the snail the strongest animal?
Because he carries a house on his back.

How do you get a squirrel down from a tree?
Act like a nut.

15

Where do you find giant snails?
At the end of giants' fingers.

What did one bee say to the other in Summer time?
'Swarm here, isn't it?'

What's the biggest mouse in the world?
A hippopotamouse!

What should you do if you
find a gorilla in your bed?
Find somewhere else to sleep!

What do you get
from nervous cows?
Milkshakes.

What did one pig say to the other?
'Let's be pen pals.'

17

Two ants were on a biscuit packet.
'Why are we running so fast?'
the first ant panted.
'Because it says "Tear along the dotted line",'
was the breathless reply.

What's the unluckiest
kind of cat to have?
A cat-astrophe.

How long are a dinosaur's legs?
Long enough to reach the ground.

What do you call a sheep with no legs?
A cloud.

How do frogs die?
They Kermit suicide.

Why was the glow-worm unhappy?
Because her children weren't very bright.

Which birds steal soap from the bath?
Robber ducks.

What's a dog's favourite hobby?
Collecting fleas.

Why did the spider buy a car?
So he could take it out for a spin!

What's green and hangs in a tree?
Giraffe snot.

Why does a giraffe have such a long neck?
Because he's got smelly feet!

What did the lion say when teaching her cubs to hunt?
'Don't go over the road until you see the zebra crossing.'

Why did the firefly keep stealing things?
Because he was light-fingered!

Distraught owner:
'Our cat's gone missing!'
Policeman:
'Why don't you put an ad in the newspaper?'
Distraught owner:
'Don't be silly –
Sooty can't read!'

ELEPHANT CORNER

Have you herd the one about the elephant?

How do you know when an elephant's hiding in your fridge? You can't shut the door.

How do you know when an elephant is under your bed? When your head touches the ceiling.

What's the best way to see a charging elephant?
On television!

How does an elephant get down from a tree?
He stands on a leaf and waits until autumn.

What do you do if you have a whole heap of cannonballs?
Give them to some bored elephants to use as marbles.

24

How does an elephant get up a tree?
He stands on an acorn and waits for it to grow.

What do you call an elephant walking through the woods?
Russell.

Why did the elephant paint its toenails red?
So it could hide upside down in a bowl of cherries.

What do you call an elephant that's small and pink?
A failure!

Why do elephants have trunks?
They'd look silly with suitcases, wouldn't they?

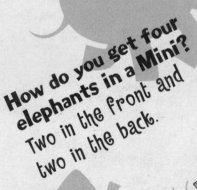

How do you get four elephants in a Mini?
Two in the front and two in the back.

How do you get a hippo in a Mini?
Chuck one of the elephants out.

How do you stop an elephant passing through the eye of a needle?
Tie a knot in his tail.

What do you call a hamster that can pick up an elephant?
Sir.

What do you call someone with an elephant on his head?
squashed.

What's red on the outside, grey on the inside and very crowded?
A bus full of elephants.

Why is an elephant large, grey and wrinkled?
If he was small, white and smooth, he'd be an aspirin.

What do you do if an elephant sits on your television?
Wait for him to get up.

Passer-by: 'One of your escaped elephants is chasing a man on a bicycle.'

Zookeeper: 'That's ridiculous. None of my elephants knows how to ride a bicycle!'

What's the difference between an elephant and a biscuit?
You can't dunk an elephant in your tea.

FISHY HUMOUR

Do your best to trawl through these ones!

What is the best way to communicate with a fish?
Drop it a line!

What did the sardine call the submarine?
A can of people!

Why did the crab go to jail?
He kept pinching things.

What do you call a fish without an eye?
A fsh!

What did the fish say when it swam into a wall?
'Dam!'

Breaking News – Brawl in Shop

A huge fight broke out in a fish and chip shop last night. A lot of fish got battered . . .

Do dolphins do things by accident?
No, they do them on porpoise!

What did the octopus say to the soldier?
'I'm armed.'

Why don't crabs share their food?
Because they are shellfish.

What fish only swims at night?
A starfish!

Why did the lobster blush?
Because the sea weed!

Which part of a fish
weighs the most?
Its scales.

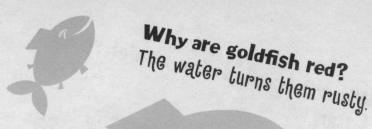

Why are goldfish red?
The water turns them rusty.

What's the difference between a fish and a piano?
You can't tuna fish.

MORE ANIMAL QUACKERS

Hare we go again!

Why does a mother kangaroo dread rainy days?
Because her children have to play indoors.

Why are parrots always clever?
Because they suck seed.

Where do hamsters come from?
Hampsterdam.

What do you call a crate of ducks?
A box of quackers.

What animals are on legal documents?
Seals.

What happened when the lion ate the comedian?
He felt funny.

What's green and squirts jam at you?
A doughnut-eating frog.

What did the neurotic pig say to the farmer?
'You take me for grunted!'

Can you name two birds that can't fly?
An ostrich and a dead parrot.

Which side of a chicken has most feathers?
The outside.

How do fleas travel?
By itch-hiking.

How do you milk a mouse?
You can't – the bucket won't fit underneath it!

How many skunks does it take to make a stink?
A phew!

How do hens dance?
Chick-to-chick.

Why don't centipedes play football?
It takes too long to put their boots on!

How do you know that bees are happy?
Because they hum while they work.

mmmmmmmmmmmmmmmmmmmmm

What animal talks a lot?
A yak.

What did the
ladybird say to the
grasshopper?
'Bug, you man me!'

How can you say 'rabbit' without
using the letter 'R'?
'Bunny.'

CROSS WORDS

Remember – no need to get cross if you don't know the answer!

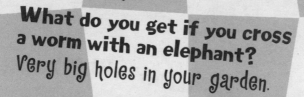

What do you get if you cross a worm with an elephant?
Very big holes in your garden.

What do you get if you cross a dog with a lion?
A terrified postman.

What do you get if you cross a spider with an elephant?
I don't know, but if you see one on the ceiling, get out of the way fast!

What do you get if you cross an elephant with a flea?
Lots of anxious dogs.

What do you get if you cross a parrot with a centipede?
A walkie-talkie.

What do you get if you cross
a cat with a bottle of vinegar?
A sour-puss.

What do you get if you cross
a sheepdog with a bunch of roses?
Collie-flowers.

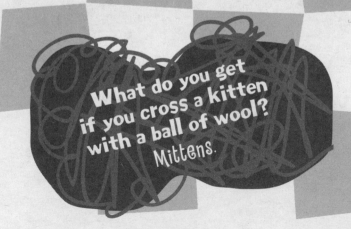

What do you get
if you cross a kitten
with a ball of wool?
Mittens.

**What do you get if you cross
a werewolf with a cow?**
A burger that bites back.

**What do you get if you cross
a flower with a lion?**
I don't know, but I wouldn't
want to smell it.

**What do you get if you
cross a boomerang with a
bottle of perfume?**
A smell you can't get rid of.

What's green, grows on trees and is scared of wolves?
The Three Little Figs.

What do you get if you cross a trout with an apartment?
A flat fish.

What do you get if you cross a ghost with a packet of crisps?
Snacks that go crunch in the night.

What do you get If you cross
a pig with a parrot?
A bird who hogs the conversation.

What do you get if you cross
a tiger with a snowman?
Frostbite.

What do you get if you
cross a cat with a shark?
A dog-less town.

What do you get if you cross a chicken with a cement mixer?

A brick layer.

What do you get if you cross a lion with a footballer?

I don't know, but when it tries to go for goal, no one stops it!

What do you get if you cross a vampire with a mummy?

Something you wouldn't want to unwrap.

What do you get if you cross loud music with an English lesson?

Punktuation.

What do you get if you cross a flying horse with a swine?

Pigasus.

What do you get if you cross a chicken with a guitar?

A hen that makes music when you pluck it.

What do you get if you cross a chicken with a dog?
A bird that lays pooched eggs.

What do you get if you cross a ghost with a chicken?
A poultry-geist.

What do you get if you cross a chicken with a bell?
An alarm cluck.

What do you get if you cross a worm with a young goat?
A dirty kid.

What do you get if you cross a chicken with a duck?
A bird that lays down.

What do you get if you cross a jellyfish with an aircraft?
A jelly-copter.

What do you get if you cross a dinosaur with a pig?
Jurassic Pork.

What do you get if you cross a nun with a barn full of chickens?
A pecking order.

What do you get if you cross a footballer with a ghost?
A ghoulie.

What do you get if you cross a couple of bananas with a pair of shoes?
Slippers.

What do you get if you cross an insect with a dance?
A cricket ball.

What do you get if you cross a sheep with a vampire?
A were-wool.

What do you get if you cross a cat with a dog?
A pet that chases itself.

What do you get if you cross a pig with a telephone?
A lot of crackling on the line.

What do you get if you cross a detective with a snake?
A spy-thon.

What do you get if you cross a biscuit with a comic strip?
Crumby jokes.

What do you get if you cross a scary creature with a high IQ?
Frank Einstein's monster.

What do you get if you cross a parrot with an elephant?
An animal that tells you everything it remembers.

What do you get if you cross a rabbit with a leek?

A bunion.

What do you get if you cross a kangaroo with an elephant?

Great big holes all over Australia.

What do you get if you cross a cat with an octagon?

An octopus.

What do you get if you cross
an insect with a reindeer?
Antlers.

What do you get if you cross a
long-haired rug with an elephant?
A great big pile in your sitting room.

What do you get if you cross a
footballer with a mythical creature?
A centaur forward.

What do you get
if you cross a fish
with two elephants?
Swimming trunks.

What do you get if you cross
a giraffe with a hedgehog?
An extra-large toothbrush.

What do you get if you cross a bear with a skunk?
Winnie the Pooh.

What do you get if you cross a unicorn with a cobbler?
A shoehorn.

CROSS THE ROAD JOKES

Even more crossed fun!

Why did the cow cross the road?
To get to the udder side.

Why did the duck cross the road?
Cos it was the chicken's day off.

Why did the chewing gum cross the road?
Cos it was stuck to the chicken.

Why did the blind chicken cross the road?
To get to the Bird's Eye shop.

Why did the chicken cross the playground?
To get to the other slide.

Why did the rooster cross the road?
To prove he wasn't chicken.

Why did the rooster cross the road?
To cock-a-doodle-doo something.

What do you call a chicken that crosses the road to roll in the dirt and then walks back?
A dirty double-crosser.

Why did the fish cross the ocean?
To get to the other tide.

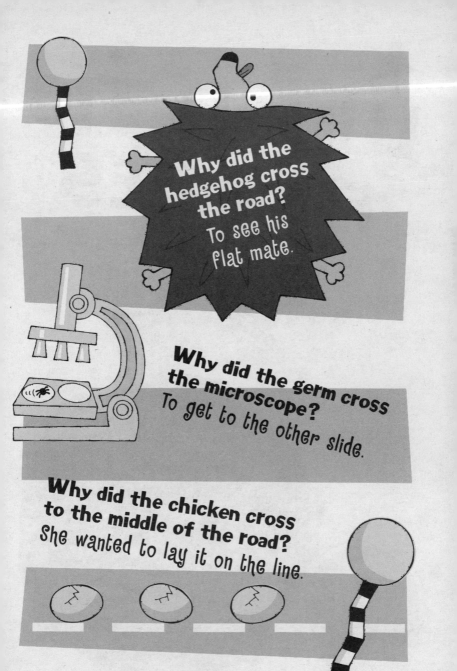

Why did the hedgehog cross the road?
To see his flat mate.

Why did the germ cross the microscope?
To get to the other slide.

Why did the chicken cross to the middle of the road?
She wanted to lay it on the line.

LUNAR-TIC FUNNIES

Watch out – these ones are outta this world!

Astronaut 1:
'I really don't like travelling faster than the speed of sound.'

Astronaut 2:
'Why? Does it make you feel ill?'

Astronaut 1:
'No. I just never catch up with what you are saying!'

How do you get directions
in deep space?
Askeroid.

How do astronauts talk to
each other in deep space?
They shout very loudly.

Which evil Star Wars hero
wears a black helmet and
goes 'quack quack'?
Duck Vader.

Science teacher: 'So, who can
tell me how fast
light travels?'
Pupil: 'I don't know, but it gets
to my house very early
each morning.'

What did the astronaut see in his frying pan?
An unidentified frying object.

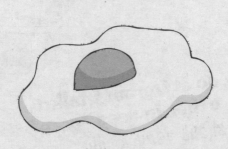

If an astronaut spits his chewing gum out of the window of his spaceship, what do you call it?
A Chew F O!

If an athlete gets athlete's foot, what does an astronaut get?
Missile toe.

Knock, knock.
Who's there?
Only Spock.
Only Spock who?
Only Spock when you're spoken to.

Knock, knock.
Who's there?
Obi Wan.
Obi Wan who?
Obi Wan a cracker?

Knock, knock.
Who's there?
Princess Leia.
Princess Leia who?
Princess Leia the couch for a nap.

What do you call a mad astronaut?
An astronut.

What kind of poetry do astronauts write when they are in space?
Uni-verses.

Living on earth makes us all space tourists. Every year, we get a free trip round the sun.

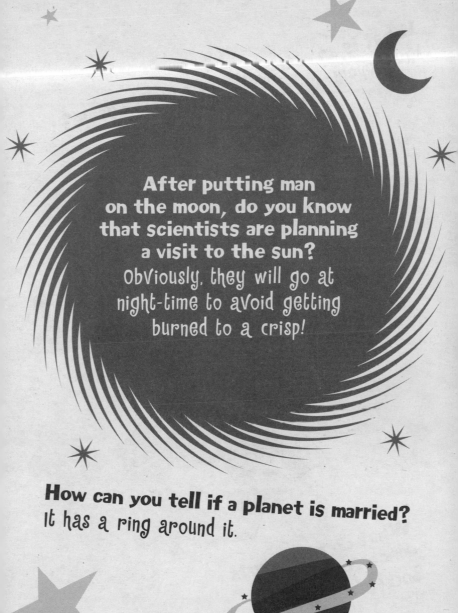

After putting man on the moon, do you know that scientists are planning a visit to the sun? Obviously, they will go at night-time to avoid getting burned to a crisp!

How can you tell if a planet is married?
It has a ring around it.

69

What is an astronaut's favourite game?
Moon-opoly.

What's the most difficult part of an astronaut's job?
Washing the (satellite) dishes.

What do astronauts dance to?
Rocket 'n' roll music.

Why did the boy become an astronaut?
Because he was no earthly good.

What do astronauts have for lunch?
Whatever is in their launch boxes.

What do astronauts wear to weddings?
Spacesuits.

What are the best days to visit space?
Moondays and Sundays.

What's the quickest way to speak to someone on Saturn?
Give them a ring.

What sort of songs do planets like to sing?
Nep-tunes.

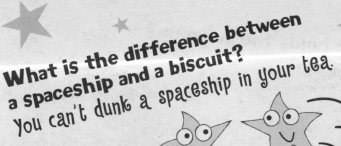

What is the difference between a spaceship and a biscuit?
You can't dunk a spaceship in your tea.

What did one shooting star say to the other?
'Pleased to meteor!'

What did the astronaut say when he saw the fleet of spaceships coming?
'Here come the spaceships!'

What holds the moon up?
Moonbeams.

All sorts of animals have been taken up into space, including dogs, monkeys and even fleas. Can you imagine a flea's spacesuit?

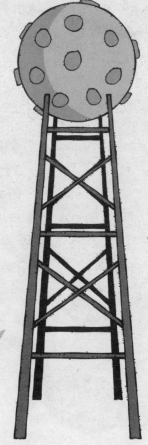

What did the moon say to the star after dinner?
'I'm pretty full.'

What is an astronaut's favourite TV show?
Countdown.

How many balls of string would it take to reach the moon?
One very large one.

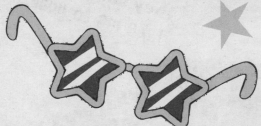

What kinds of stars wear glasses?
Movie stars.

ALIEN ABSURDITIES

Aliens are just as silly as us, you know!

How can you tell Martians are excellent gardeners?
Because of their green thumbs.

What did the aliens say when they landed in the flower bed?
'Take me to your weeder.'

What are the slowest creatures on the moon?
Snail-iens.

Why does Superman hate new technology?
Have you ever tried to change into a blue suit and cape behind a mobile phone?

What does Captain Kirk say on Halloween?
'Trek or treat.'

Why was the slimy alien so pleased with himself?
He got listed in Ooze Who.

What does an alien put on his toast?
Mars-malade.

How do you know if an alien is in your house?
When there is a spaceship parked in your garden.

Where do aliens keep fish they capture from other planets?
In a planetarium.

Why are spacemen such good party guests?
They have a blast.

How do solar systems hold up their trousers?
With an asteroid belt.

Where do aliens go after they get married?
On their honeyearth.

Where do aliens go on holiday?
Lanzarocket.

Why didn't the alien school have any computers?
Because someone ate all the apples.

What do aliens dress up as on Halloween?
Humans.

Why was the thirsty alien hanging around the computer?
He was looking for the space bar.

How does a Martian know when he's attractive?
When bits of metal stick to him.

Why do some aliens make their spaceships out of twisted planks of wood?
So they can travel at warp speed.

What do aliens hit in
a game of badminton?
Shuttlecocks.

If a flying saucer is an aircraft,
does that make a flying broomstick
a witchcraft?

How do you confuse an alien?
Give him a piece of paper with 'PTO'
written on both sides.

What is it called when a
Martian has perfect vision?
20/20/20/20

A man was trying to explain to an alien what life is like on Earth. The alien pointed at an apple tree and asked what the fruit was hanging off the branches.

'An apple,' said the man.

The alien pointed at a worm wriggling on the ground, and asked what it was.

'A worm,' replied the man.

'What's the difference?' asked the alien.

The man paused, thinking hard.

'Well,' said the man, 'have you ever had a worm pie?'

What sort of sweets do Martians eat?
Martian mallows.

What disease did everyone on the *Enterprise* catch?
Chicken Spocks.

Why did the alien jump in the water when it started raining?
So he wouldn't get wet.

What did the alien say to the petrol pump?
'Take your finger out of your ear when I am talking to you!'

What do you get if you cross a spaceship with a chef?
A flying sauce-r.

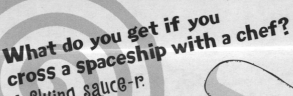

How do you know when an alien has been in your fridge?
When there are three footprints in the butter.

If Martians live on Mars and Venusians live on Venus, what lives on Pluto?
Fleas.

85

How do aliens throw an intergalactic space party? They planet.

Where do aliens go on holiday? Greenland.

What do you do if you see a spaceman? Park in it, man!

Where do aliens get their eggs?
From a little green hen.

What's the most popular name for a pub on Mars?
The Mars Bar.

What do you call a sad spaceship?
An unidentified crying object.

Where does Doctor Who
go to get his salami?
The dalek-atessan.

How do aliens get their
baby to fall asleep?
They rocket.

Who's green, 'mad for it'
and lives on Mars?
Alien Gallagher.

Where do Martians go
to watch movies?
Cine-mars.

What's small, green and
silver, and goes up and down?
An alien in a lift.

What did the hungry alien
say when it landed on Earth?
'Take me to your larder.'

What goes in one year and out the other?
A time machine.

Did you hear about the man who was kidnapped by extra-terrestrial teddy bears?
He had a close encounter of the furred kind.

Why do aliens have such terrible trouble drinking tea?
Because of the flying saucers.

Why don't aliens like Christmas?
Because they don't like giving away their presence.

What do you call an overweight ET?
An extra-cholesterol!

What should you do if you find a green alien?
Wait until it is ripe.

What do you give a sick alien?
Planet-cetamol.

When do you find toilets in space?
Only once in a loo moon.

What do you call a magician in space?
A flying sorcerer.

Alien child: 'Mum, I'm so hungry. When are we going to eat?'

Alien mother: 'Pipe down. Can't you see I've only got two pairs of hands?'

Where do aliens catch the bus from?
The space station.

How do you know when there is an alien under your bed?
When there is a green light coming from underneath it.

Knock, knock.
Who's there?
Aileen.
Aileen who?
Aileen from outer space!

Knock, knock.
Who's there?
Juicy.
Juicy who?
Juicy that alien waving?

BARMY BIRTHDAYS

Surprisingly stupid jokes about everyone's special day.

A little boy and his sister rang their grandma on her birthday. They both sang 'Happy Birthday' down the phone, their parents joining in.

'I think you have the wrong number,' a male voice said at the other end.

The family were horrified.

'Don't worry,' the stranger said. 'You need all the practice you can get.'

What does every birthday end with? The letter 'y'.

Why couldn't the Stone Age man send birthday cards? Have you ever tried sticking a stamp on a rock?

What happened at Moby Dick's birthday party? He had a whale of a time.

'For my birthday, I'd like a dress to match the colour of my eyes,' Rebecca said wistfully.

'Blimey! Where am I going to get a bloodshot dress?' her brother asked.

What goes up
and never
comes down?
your age!

Frazzled mother: 'How are we going
to blow up all these
balloons for Gwyneth's
birthday party?'

Helpful son: 'With a pin?'

'Was there anyone famous
born on your birthday?'
'No, only small babies.'

What do you say to cows on their birthday?
'Happy birthday to moo.'

What do you say to a cat on his birthday?
'Happy birthday to miaow.'

What do you say to a parrot on its birthday?
'Happy birdy to you.'

How does a mussel celebrate her birthday?
She shell-ebrates!

'I found the perfect thing for your birthday . . . No-thing!'

Did you hear about
the stupid boy who
tried to make his sister
a birthday cake?
The candles melted
in the oven.

Where would you find a present for your cat's birthday?
In a cat-alogue.

What do trees and dogs have in common on their birthdays?
You can say happy bark-day to both.

What did one candle say to the other candle?
'Don't birthdays burn you up?'

What's your favourite
type of present?
Another one.

Granny

We didn't put
candles on Granny's
birthday cake this year.
We wanted to help
the environment.

'Birthday cake gives me heartburn.'
'Try taking off the candles.'

Father: 'Do you like your **AM radio?**'
Son: 'Yes, thanks. I just wish I had a radio I could also play in the evening.'

Grandmother: 'Do you like your pocket calculator?'
Granddaughter: 'Yes, thanks. It will come in useful for figuring out how many pockets I have got.'

Why did the woman feel warm on her birthday in December?
Cos everyone kept on toasting her.

Why did the little boy stand on his head at the party?
Because he knew there was an upside-down cake.

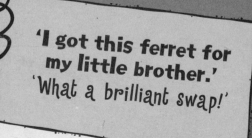

'I got this ferret for my little brother.'
'What a brilliant swap!'

MONSTER MADNESS

Scarily funny jokes about witches, ghouls, mummies and other strange beasties!

Who's the meanest ape?
Gorilla the Hun.

Who is the meanest octopus in the old West?
Billy the Squid.

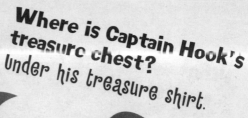

Where is Captain Hook's treasure chest?
Under his treasure shirt.

What do you call a monster with a pair of socks in his ears?
Anything you like — he can't hear you.

What do you say when King Kong graduates from university?
'Kong-gratulations!'

What goes chomp, chomp, ouch!
A monster with a bad tooth.

Where do ghosts like to go on holiday?
The Dead Sea.

If you crossed a Tyrannosaurus rex, what would you get?
Eaten.

Mummy monster: 'Darling, did you wake up grumpy this morning?'

Baby monster: 'No, I think Dad woke himself up.'

Why don't zombies get more invitations?
Because they are never the life of the party.

What do you call a monster that devours everything in its path?
Lonely.

Did you hear about the invisible man
who had children?
He lost them.

What did the boy monster say to the
girl monster?
'I want to hold your hand, hand, hand . . .'

Why should you never upset a cannibal?
You might get into hot water.

What does a ghost use to go hunting?
A boo and arrow.

How do ghosts begin letters?
'Tomb it may concern . . .'

Why didn't the ghost go to the dance?
He had no-body to go with.

How do you address Count Dracula?
Very politely.

What is Dracula's favourite sport?
Casketball.

Who is Dracula most likely to fall in love with?
The girl necks door.

How does Dracula help a baseball team?
By turning into a bat.

What is Dracula's favourite milkshake flavour?
Vein-illa.

What is Dracula's least-favourite meal?
Stake and three veg.

Did you hear about the ghostly boomerang?
It kept on coming back to haunt people.

How do vampires kiss?
Very carefully.

How did the vampire race end?
Neck and neck.

What do vampires drink
when they wake up?
Coffin-ated beverages.

What do vampires sing
on New Year's Eve?
'Auld Fang Syne.'

What did one vampire
say to the other?
'You're bats!'

**What did one zombie say
to the other?**
'Get a life!'

What do baby ghosts chew?
Boo-ble gum.

**What do you call a monster
with no neck?**
The Lost Neck Monster.

114

What's the best way to stop a stinky swamp monster from smelling?
Hold its nose.

What are two things a troll can't eat for breakfast?
Lunch and dinner.

What do you do if an ogre runs off with your football?
Buy another one.

115

What's the definition of a cannibal?
Someone who goes into a restaurant and orders the waiter.

On which day do cannibals eat people?
Chewsday.

How did the cannibal congratulate his friend?
By toasting him.

What's a cannibal's favourite game?
Swallow the leader.

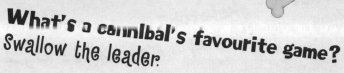

What kind of monster loves to dance?
The boogieman.

Why did the zombie get arrested for eating muesli?
They thought he was a cereal killer.

What is a skeleton?
Bones with the people scraped off.

Why did the skeleton cross the road?
To get to the spare parts shop.

What is a ghoul's favourite amusement park ride?
The roller-ghoster.

What is a skeleton's favourite instrument?
A trom-bone.

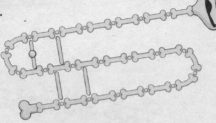

Why are skeletons so calm?
Nothing gets under their skin.

What is the difference between a musician and a corpse?
One composes, and the other decomposes.

What game does Godzilla like best?
Squash.

What did Godzilla say before attacking his victims?
'Nice to heat you.'

What was the scariest dinosaur?
The terror-dactyl.

Did you hear about the monster that went to the beauty parlour?
They wouldn't let her in.

 # A Ghoulish Library

Good House-Creeping
by Polt R. Geist

Fangs for the Memories
by Vamp Ire

Grave Expectations
by G. Host

Popular Coffin' Cures
by Dr Acula

Have a Rattling Good Time
by S. Keleton

My Life with Dracula
by I. Drew Blood

Confessions of a Werewolf
by Ripu Tashreds

Swallowing my Pride
by Canni Bell Lion

How to Survive a Vampire Attack
by I. M. Fein

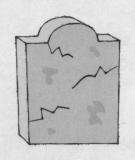

What did the zombie say when it buried its victim?
'You're in deep trouble now.'

How do ghouls dance?
Shriek-to-shriek.

What goes round a cemetery but doesn't move?
A fence.

Why was the cemetery crowded?
Cos everyone was dying to get in.

How do you tell when a mummy is sick?
He's all stuffed up.

Who does a mummy take on a date?
Anybody he can dig up.

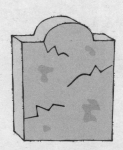

123

What's the best way to talk to a mummy?
From a long, long way away!

Why did the mummy refuse to go on holiday?
He didn't want to unwind.

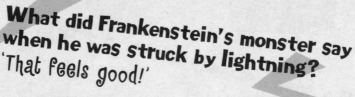

What did Frankenstein's monster say when he was struck by lightning?
'That feels good!'

What are a ghost's parents called?
Trans-parents.

How do ghosts like their eggs?
Terri-fried.

Why didn't the boy ghoul ask the girl ghoul out?
He didn't stand a ghost of a chance.

What happened when the tree saw the ghost?
It was petrified.

What does a good-looking ghost look like?
Very hauntsome.

What is the best way for a ghost hunter to keep fit?
By exorcising regularly.

How do ghosts predict their futures?
They read their horror-scopes.

Did you hear about the stupid ghost?
He climbed over walls.

Why do monsters have wrinkles?
Have you ever tried to iron a monster?

Where do ghosts take their letters?
To the ghost office.

Why do witches fly on broomsticks?
Because their vacuum cleaners don't have long-enough cords.

What's the most important rule for witches?
Don't fly off the handle.

What do witches wear to bed?
Fright-gowns.

What do you call a witch made from cotton with lots of holes and a handle?
A string hag.

What subject do witches enjoy at school?
Spelling.

What goes cackle, cackle, bonk?
A witch laughing her head off.

**How do witches keep
their hair in place?**
With scare spray.

What do you call a witch's garage?
A broom cupboard.

What do you call a witch
who lives by the beach?
A sand-witch.

What
do schools
do to naughty
witches?
They ex-spell them.

What did the witch ask for
when she booked into the hotel?
'A broom with a view.'

How many witches does it take to change a light bulb?
Just one, but she changes it into a toad.

What kind of mail does a witch prefer?
Hex-press delivery.

Where is the witch's temple?
On either side of her forehead.

What is the difference between a witch and the letters

M
A
K
E
S
?

One makes spells and the other spells 'makes'.

Why do witches wear pointy hats?
To keep their pointy heads warm.

Why is a witch like a candle?
They are both wicked.

What's evil and ugly and goes up and down all day?
A witch stuck in a lift.

What happens when you see twin witches?
You aren't able to tell which witch is which.

What do you get if you put a witch in the fridge?
A cold spell.

134

Why couldn't the witch sing Christmas carols?
Because of the frog in her throat.

How do you make a witch itch?
Take away the 'w'.

Why do witches get really good bargains?
Cos they like to haggle.

How do witches like to take their tea while on their broomsticks?
With flying saucers.

What do witches say when they overtake each other?
'Broom, broom, broom!'

What's the first thing a wizard does in the morning?
He wakes up.

Why did Dr Frankenstein cry?
He'd broken up with his ghoul-friend.

Did you hear about the boy who was so scared of Halloween he went trick or treating by phone . . .

Baby dragon: 'Mummy, I had a terrible dream a man in a tin suit was chasing me!'

Mummy dragon: 'There, there, dear – it was only a knightmare.'

How does a werewolf
sign his letters?
'Best Vicious . . .'

What did one ghost say to
the other ghost?
'Do you believe in people?'

One ghost was telling a tall tale to a
group of his captivated ghost friends:
'And then I sliced off his head, and
at the same time thrust his sword
through my heart.'
'A likely tale,' sniffed one ghost.
'I can see right through you!'

Why are dinosaurs healthier than dragons?
Because dinosaurs don't smoke.

What do you do when dozens of zombies surround your house?
Hope it's Halloween . . .

When do ghosts have breakfast?
Sometime in the moaning.

A boy went to a Halloween party with a sheet on his head. 'Are you a ghost?' his friend asked. 'No, I'm an unmade bed,' came the reply.

Who writes ghost movies?
A crypt writer

How do monsters count to twenty-three?
On their fingers.

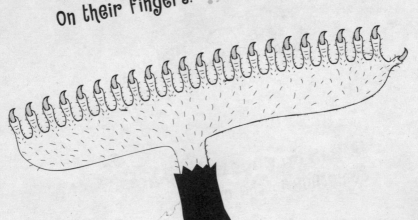

What did the monster say to his girlfriend?
'Hello, gore-juice!'

When do werewolves go trick or treating?
On Howl-o-ween.

HAPPY FAMILIES

You can't choose your family, but you can choose to chuckle at this lot!

'You'll never get that dog to obey you.'
'Rubbish. Remember how stubborn you were when I first married you?'

'My little brother keeps on bumping into things.'
'I thought he didn't look too good.'

142

What sort of clothes does the family dog wear?
Pet-ticoats.

Little Elijah was stroking his new kitten when the kitten began to purr. 'Mummy!' Elijah shouted. 'Come quickly! Kitty is starting to boil!'

'I used to work with thousands under me!' Grandpa said to his wide-eyed grandchildren. 'Really? Where did you work?' little Rachel asked. 'At the cemetery.'

143

Woman 1: 'That man over there must be the most unattractive person here.'

Woman 2: 'That's my husband.'

Woman 1: 'Oh dear, I am sorry.'

Woman 2: 'You're sorry? How do you think I feel?'

'How was your holiday to Switzerland?' the teacher asked Jake. 'Was the scenery lovely?'

'I don't know.' Jake said glumly. 'The mountains kept on getting in the way.'

Wife: 'Darling, why are you cutting up that block of ice?'

Husband: 'So it will fit into the ice-cube tray, of course!'

Rhonda: 'Our cat is worth £300!'

Liesel: 'Gosh, how can a cat save so much money?'

A little boy got separated from his father at the funfair.
'What's your father like?' the kindly attendant asked.
'Football and going to the pub,' the small boy said matter-of-factly.

'OK, so where is the drip?' the plumber asked.
'Oh, he's in the bathroom trying to fix the leak,' said the cross housewife.

Jim: 'My family lives in a nudist colony.'

Tim: 'Gosh, that must make Halloween quite a let-down.'

Teenager 1: 'It must be hard being a turtle.'

Teenager 2: 'Why?'

Teenager 1: 'Cos you can't run away from home!'

'Why do you want to work in a bank, Jimmy?'
'Cos there's money in it!'

'I've changed my mind.'
'Finally! Does the new one work any better?'

'Men just don't want to get married these days,' lamented one girl to another.
How do you know? asked her friend
'I've asked so many of them!'

'**Why won't you take your little brother to the zoo?**'
'If they want him, they can come and get him!'

What did the father firefly say every morning before going to work?
'Bye, I'm glowing now!'

'**We're going to have the rooster for dinner,**' said the farmer to his family. 'Cool,' said the youngest child. 'Can we teach it to hold a knife and fork?'

'My new baby sister just lost two pounds.'
'Is she sick?'
'No, we just changed her nappy.'

'Darling, why have you got a sausage behind your ear?'
'Oh dear, I must have eaten my pencil for breakfast!'

Amy had just got her driving licence and was out on her first drive. Her mother called her on her mobile phone, begging her to be careful as she had just heard that there was a crazed motorist driving the wrong way on the M25.

'What do you mean, there is ONE crazy motorist?' a flustered Amy shouted from the roadside. 'There's hundreds of them!'

Son: 'Dad, I'm going to call your dance the Lift.'

Father: 'Why?'

Son: 'Because it hasn't got any steps!'

'I don't think my mum is a very good mother,' confided one small child to his friend.

'Why's that?'

'Cos she keeps getting me up when I'm sleepy, and putting me to bed when I'm wide awake!'

zzzzzzzzzzzzzzzzzzzzzzzzzzzzz

Wife: 'Why has the clock stopped working?'

Husband: 'I guess its time is up.'

'Shall I tell you the joke about the jam?'
'You'd better not — I'll spread it around.'

When should you check for a puncture?
Every time there is a fork in the road.

Sister: **'Why have you got a light bulb on your head?'**
Brother: 'I'm just trying to get some bright ideas for my essay.'

'My parents left me an only child.'
'What did you do?'
'What do you think I did?
I raised her like she was my sister.'

'Mum, the dog's been
naughty again. There's
a poodle on the carpet.'

When should you put a spider
in your sister's bed?
When you can't find a frog.

My brother is so dumb he thinks that barnacles are where seahorses live.

'When I grow up, I'm going to marry the boy next door.'
'How sweet! Do you like him, then?'
'Not really. It's just that I'm not allowed to cross the road.'

A little boy was watching his big sister cover her face in cream before going to bed. Transfixed, he asked her,
'What's that for?'
'To make me beautiful,' she replied, smiling.
'It doesn't work, does it?'

'I flew to New Zealand!'
said the returning gap student.
'Wow. Didn't that make your arms tired?'
asked his little brother.

What song did
they play when
the baker
got married?
Here crumbs
the bride.

'Daddy, I ate the dictionary!'
'Don't breathe a word to your mother!'

Did you hear about the stupid investment banker? He bought a BMW instead of a Lamborghini because he can spell 'BMW'.

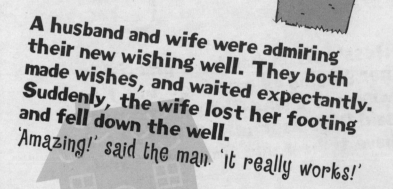

A husband and wife were admiring their new wishing well. They both made wishes, and waited expectantly. Suddenly, the wife lost her footing and fell down the well. 'Amazing!' said the man. 'It really works!'

Sister: 'I'm on a new diet – the pasta diet.'

Brother: 'How does it work?'

Sister: 'Every time I get hungry I walk right pasta fridge.'

Two small children went into their parents' bathroom. 'Whatever you do, don't step on that,' said the eldest, pointing at the scales. 'Why not?'
'Because every time Mummy steps on it, she screams.'

Ross's sister had been practising her singing all morning. 'Sis, I'd wish you'd sing Christmas carols,' said Ross wistfully. 'Then I'd only have to hear you sing once a year.'

'Dad, can you do my maths homework with me?'
'I don't think it would be right.'
'True, but you could at least have a go!'

'So, do you like your new job at the duvet factory?'
'There's nowhere to go but down.'

'Billy, stop pulling the cat's tail!'
'But she's the one doing all the pulling!'

Why did the grandpa tiptoe past the bathroom?
He didn't want to wake the sleeping pills.

159

'Can you help me?' a worried mother asked the animal shelter officer. 'I'm looking for a stray cat with one eye.'

'Would it help if you used both eyes?' yawned the officer

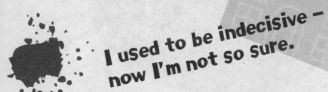

I used to be indecisive – now I'm not so sure.

I got into really hot water last night. I took a bath.

'How do you like your new job at the Centre for Communicable Diseases?'

'It makes me sick.'

I call my girlfriend 'Plum' because she has a heart of stone.

The Dunce family were driving to see Stonehenge. They saw a sign saying 'Stonehenge left'. They were very disappointed and drove home.

'I'm very lucky I'm not vain. Most girls as good-looking as I am are, you see.'

'Go next door to play. Your father isn't able to read his paper.'
'Really? I can read it and I'm only ten!'

'It's amazing. Today you can telephone from an aeroplane!' said the elderly infrequent flyer.
'Of course you can – anyone can tell a phone from a plane!' said her bemused companion.

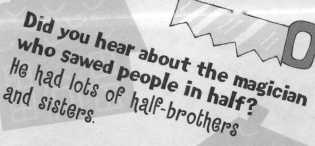

Did you hear about the magician who sawed people in half? He had lots of half-brothers and sisters.

An elderly grandfather wanted to visit his daughter who lived in Australia. He rang the airline and asked how long it would take. 'Just a minute,' came the reply. He thanked the airline employee and hung up.

'How old is your grandad?'
'Hmm, I'm not sure, but he's been around for a long time.'

How did the invisible boy upset his father?
He kept on appearing.

'When I grow up, I want to be a ballet dancer!' said Cindy proudly.
'That'll keep you on your toes,' said her absent-minded father.

Did you hear about the untidy student?
He was such a slob, even the cockroaches moved out.

Did you hear about the caterpillars that got married?
It was larva at first sight.

Did you hear about the little girl who was named after her grandmother?
She was called Gran.

Did you hear about the boy who was called Fog?
He was dense and wet.

How many brothers does it take to wallpaper a room?
Only one - if you slice him very finely.

'Why has this pot boiled dry? Didn't I ask you to notice when it boiled over?'
'I did, Mum! It happened at 7:30!'

'I feel like going to bed!' yawned Nicola.
'Why, because everyone keeps turning you down?' ribbed her brother.

'I bet I can lift an elephant with three fingers!' boasted Andrew to his friend Christian.
'Prove it!'
'Show me an elephant with three fingers and I'll be glad to.'

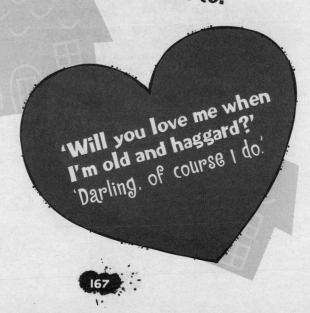

'Will you love me when I'm old and haggard?'
'Darling, of course I do.'

'I've got skin like a peach!'
'Who wants to have skin like a sixteen-year-old peach?'

'Mum, there's a lady at the door who is collecting for the new swimming pool!'
'Ask her if she wants a glass of water!'

SCHOOL DAZE

Giggles galore will help you get through a long day at school!

'How do you spell "chrysanthemum"?'

'C-r-i-s-a-n-t-h-i-m-o-om.'

'That's not how the dictionary spells it.'

'You didn't ask me how the dictionary spells it!'

Teacher: 'Does anyone know what an archaeologist is?'

Jill: 'It's someone whose career is in ruins.'

Teacher: 'Tommy, what's the most important thing you have learnt in chemistry?'

Tommy: 'Never lick the spoon.'

What happened when the wheel was invented? It caused a revolution.

Why was King Arthur always tired? He had an awful lot of sleepless knights.

What's a mushroom? The place where they keep the school dinners.

Why did the schoolboy come out of the toilets smiling? He was flushed with success.

The maths classroom was getting awfully stuffy. One boy raised his hand and asked if he could open the window. 'Just a fraction,' came the stern reply.

Where was the Magna Carta signed?
At the bottom.

What is black and white and extremely difficult?
An exam paper.

Sayed: 'Mum, the teacher shouted at me for something I didn't do!'

Mother: 'What was that?'

Sayed: 'My homework!'

Head teacher: 'Do you know how many teachers work at this school?'

Peter: 'About a quarter of them, it seems.'

Johnny: 'I'm never going to smoke – it's so bad for your health!'

Jerome: 'I know – just look at what happened to all the dragons!'

Why is a teacher like a hiker?
Cos they both ramble on.

Teacher: 'Don't whistle while you're working.'

Rhodri: 'Oh, I'm not working, just whistling.'

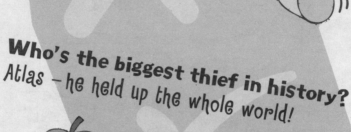

Who's the biggest thief in history?
Atlas – he held up the whole world!

Why was the head teacher worried?
Because there were so many rulers in the school.

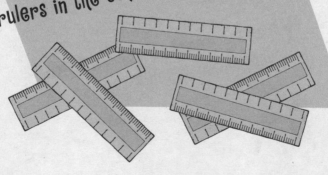

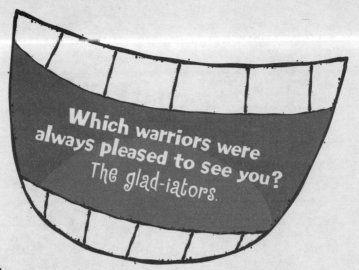

Which warriors were always pleased to see you?
The glad-iators.

Where does a pig keep his books?
In his mucksack.

Boy 1: 'So where are you from?'
Boy 2: 'Glasgow.'
Boy 1: 'Which part?'
Boy 2: 'All of me, actually.'

Teacher: 'What's the capital of Norway?'

Mohammed: '"N", I expect.'

Teacher: 'How much is half of eight?'

Toby: 'Which way?'

Teacher: 'What do you mean, "which way"?'

Toby: 'Well, up and down makes three and across makes nought.'

What's the difference between a book and a teacher? You can shut a book up.

How do bees get to school?
By school buzz.

When Rhonda left school,
she was filled with regret.
She was sorry she ever had to go.

Which famous painting
never stopped complaining?
The Moaner Lisa.

Why were ancient sailing ships environmentally friendly?
Because they could always go hundreds of miles to the galleon!

Why was the book upset?
It was left on the shelf.

Teacher: 'Kumari, do you have to come to school chewing gum?'
Kumari: 'No, miss. I could stay at home and chew it there instead!'

Which mountain is always on the go?
Mount Never-rest.

**What's black when clean
and white when dirty?**
A blackboard.

**What was the blackbird
doing in the school library?**
Looking for bookworms.

Mother: 'Did you have any problems with your French on your school trip to Paris?'

Hermione: 'No, but the French certainly did.'

Teacher: 'If you had to divide 624 by twelve, what would you get?'

Tom: 'The wrong answer.'

What did one maths textbook say to the other?
'Boy, have I got problems!'

Teacher: 'If your father earned £1,500 a week and gave your mother half, what would she have?'

Jacqui: 'A heart attack.'

Teacher: 'Linda, if I had six oranges in my right hand and ten in my left, what would I have?'

Linda: 'Huge hands, miss.'

How did knights make chain mail?

From steel wool.

Teacher: 'That essay you wrote on "My Cat" is the same as your sister's.'

Cheryl: 'It should be! It's the same cat.'

Teacher: 'Who can tell me what seven times five is?'

Eoghan: 'Thirty-five.'

Teacher: 'That's good.'

Eoghan: 'Good? That was perfect!'

?

Teacher: 'When you yawn you should put your hand in front of your mouth.'

Ian: 'What! And get bitten?'

How did the Vikings communicate with one another?
Norse code.

How does the teacher keep his class on its toes?
He puts drawing pins on their chairs.

Why is homework always boring?
It makes holes in your free time.

Lisa: 'I'm doing really well at school.'

Mother: 'That's wonderful, darling!'

Lisa: 'Yes, today I was first in the lunch queue!'

I really don't like my new school. The teacher doesn't know a thing – all he does is ask questions!

Boy 1: 'I think my teacher's good because she doesn't have a pet.'

Boy 2: 'Yes, she does, she has a dog.'

Teacher: 'Now, for homework, I'd like you to write me an essay on Hadrian's Wall.'

Belinda: 'Please, miss, I'd rather write on paper!'

Why did Robin Hood steal from the rich?
Because the poor didn't have anything worth stealing.

Mother: 'Does your teacher like you?'
Daughter: 'Well, I think so. She keeps on putting kisses on my homework!'

English teacher: 'What word is always spelt incorrectly?'

Keisha: 'Incorrectly!'

Why did Henry VIII have so many wives?
He liked to chop and change!

What did the paper say to the pencil?
'Write on!'

What does an elf do after school?
Gnome-work!

Which queen burped a lot?
Queen Hic-toria.

What musical instruments do Spanish fishermen play?
Cast-a-nets.

Where are traitors beheaded?
Just above the shoulders.

History teacher: 'Max, were the
pyramids built by
the Egyptians?'
Max: 'Um, I sphinx so!'

Teacher: 'Hugo, I think your father
has been helping you with
your homework.'
Hugo: 'No, he hasn't –
he did it all himself!'

What do you get if you cross a famous warrior with a fruit?
Alexander the Grape.

What do Attila the Hun and Winnie the Pooh have in common?
The!

Why is the Amazon river so relaxed?
It just goes with the flow.

Why should a school never
be near a chicken farm?
So the pupils can't hear fowl language.

Teacher: 'You, boy, name me
two pronouns.'
Boy: 'Who, me?'
Teacher: 'Correct.'

Teacher: 'Why are you late, Katy?'
Katy: 'Because of a sign down the road.'
Teacher: 'What does a sign have to
do with your being late?'
Katy: 'The sign said,
"School ahead, go slow"!'

Teacher: 'Please don't talk while you are doing your exam.'
Pupil: 'Don't worry, we aren't doing the exam, we're just talking.'

What's the first thing Henry VIII did on ascending the throne?
He sat down.

Father: 'Nick, what does this F mean in your report?'
Nick: 'Oh, F means fantastic!'

Teacher: 'I hope I didn't see you looking at Tom's exam paper.'

Pupil: 'I hope you didn't too!'

Mother: 'What did you learn in school today?'

Son: 'Not nearly enough – I've got to go back tomorrow . . .'

What does 'minimum' mean?
A very small mother.

What do we do with crude oil?
Teach it some manners.

Girl: 'I'm learning ancient history.'
Boy: 'So am I. Let's talk over old times!'

Tina: 'What are you going to be when you leave school?'
Sarah: 'An old, old lady.'

A man escaped from prison by digging a hole from his cell to the outside world. When he finally emerged he found himself in the middle of the pre-school playground. 'I'm free, I'm free!' he shouted.

'So what?' said one little girl. 'I'm four!'

Where were most monarchs crowned?
On the head.

If there are ten cats in a boat and one jumps out, how many are left?
None. They are all copycats.

Who was the scariest nurse ever?
Florence Frightingale.

Father: 'How do you like going to school?'

Son: 'The going bit is fine, as is the coming home bit, but I'm not too keen on the bit in between!'

Why were the teacher's eyes crossed?
Because she couldn't control her pupils.

When did King Henry VIII die?
Just before they buried him.

What is the Great Depression?
When you get a bad report card.

How do you spell 'hard water' with three letters?
I-C-E.

If a bottle of lemonade became a teacher, what subject would it teach? Fizzical education!

The Best Excuses for Not Doing Your Homework

I lost my homework fighting a kid who said you were the worst teacher in the school.

I didn't want to add to your already heavy workload.

My little sister ate it.

Aliens from outer space took it in order to discover how the human mind works.

Our heating has stopped working, so we had to burn it to keep warm.

Which king had a noisy bottom?
Richard the Lionfart.

Teacher: 'Class, we are having only half a day of school this morning.'

Class: 'Hooray!'

Teacher: 'Then we will have the other half this afternoon.'

What is the centre of gravity?
The letter 'V'.

198

What's the longest word in the English language?
Smiles – because there is a mile between the first and last letters.

Teacher: 'Your homework seems to be in your father's handwriting.'

Ravi: 'Yes, I used his pen.'

Teacher: 'You missed school yesterday, didn't you?'

Sam: 'No, not a bit!'

Pupil 1: 'I could be on the school football team if it weren't for two things!'

Pupil 2: 'Oh yes, what's that?'

Pupil 1: 'My feet!'

School nurse: 'Have you ever had trouble with pneumonia?'

Pupil: 'Only when I've had to spell it!'

Why was nobody able to play cards on Noah's Ark?

Because Noah was standing on the deck.

Which of Shakespeare's plays was about a bacon factory?
Hamlet.

Did you hear about the boy who was sent out of his tennis class?
He was making a racket.

What book has the most stirring chapters?
A cook book.

Jamie will make a very good astronomer when he leaves school. He's always staring into space.

Teacher: 'Make a sentence starting with the letter 'I'.'
Chris: 'I is . . .'
Teacher: 'No, I am . . .'
Chris: 'OK. I am the ninth letter of the alphabet.'

What does the word 'abundance' mean?
Lots of dancing cakes.

Parent: 'Amit, why does your maths exam have a big zero on it?'

Amit: 'It's not a zero. The teacher ran out of stars and she gave me a moon instead!'

Teacher: 'Be sure to go straight home.'

Susie: 'I can't, I live round the corner!'

What came after the Stone Age?
The saus-age!

What kind of food do maths teachers eat?
Square meals.

What's the best place to have the sickroom at school?
Next to the canteen!

Why was the school soup rich?
Because it had twenty-four carrots in it!

Pupil: 'There are feathers in the custard.'

School cook: 'Well, it is Bird's Custard!'

Teacher: 'Name three famous Poles.'

Pupil: 'North, South and tad.'

Pupil: 'This egg is bad!'

School cook: 'Don't blame me, I only laid the table!'

If Ireland sank into the sea, which county wouldn't sink?
Cork.

What is a volcano? A mountain with hiccups!

Why did the teacher call both her sons Ed?
Because she thought two Eds would be better than one.

Where do geologists go for entertainment?
To a rock concert.

What is the best hand to write with?
Neither – it is best to write with a pen.

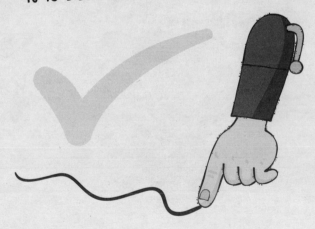

Which Elizabethan sailor could stop bicycles?
Sir Francis Brake.

KNOCK, KNOCK

You'll be answering the door with a grin with these gags!

Knock, knock.
Who's there?
Colleen.
Colleen who?
Colleen yourself up, you're a mess!

Knock, knock.
Who's there?
Romeo.
Romeo who?
Romeover the river, please!

Knock, knock.
Who's there?
Chester.
Chester who?
Chester drawers.

Knock, knock.
Who's there?
Alfie.
Alfie who?
Alfie terrible if you go!

Knock, knock.
Who's there?
Douglas.
Douglas who?
Douglas is broken.

Knock, knock.
Who's there?
Noah.
Noah who?
Noah accounting for taste.

Knock, knock.
Who's there?
Alec.
Alec who?
Alec a big hug.

Knock, knock.
Who's there?
Liz.
Liz who?
**Liz see what
you look like!**

Knock, knock.
Who's there?
Cows go.
Cows go who?
No, cows go moo!

Knock, knock.
Who's there?
Repeat.
Repeat who?
Who who who!

Knock, knock.
Who's there?
Daisy.
Daisy who?
Daisy plays, night he sleeps.

211

Knock, knock.
Who's there?
Archie.
Archie who?
Bless you!

Knock, knock.
Who's there?
Yule.
Yule who?
Yule never know!

Knock, knock.
Who's there?
Heywood.
Heywood who?
Heywood you open the door?

Knock, knock.
Who's there?
Nanny.
Nanny who?
Knock, knock.
Who's there?
Nanny.
Nanny who?
Knock, knock.
Who's there?
Auntie.
Auntie who?
Auntie you glad
it wasn't Nanny!

Knock, knock.
Who's there?
Ben.
Ben who?
Ben Dover.

Knock, knock.
Who's there?
Sean.
Sean who?
Sean Lamb.

Knock, knock.
Who's there?
Renata.
Renata who?
Renata sugar. Can I borrow some?

Knock, knock.
Who's there?
Bella.
Bella who?
Bella not working, that's why I knocked!

Knock, knock.
Who's there?
Jean.
Jean who?
Jeanius – you just
don't recognize it!

Knock, knock.
Who's there?
Alvin.
Alvin who?
Alvin a fabulous time,
how about you?

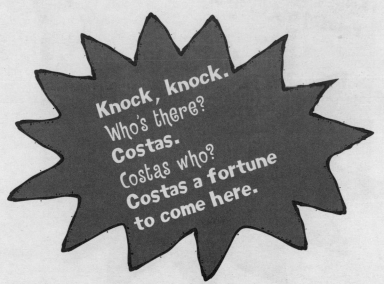

Knock, knock.
Who's there?
Costas.
Costas who?
Costas a fortune
to come here.

215

Knock, knock.
Who's there?
Jester.
Jester who?
Jester minute –
I'm trying to find my keys!

Knock, knock.
Who's there?
Falafel.
Falafel who?
Falafel my bike and it really hurt!

Knock, knock.
Who's there?
Juan.
Juan who?
Juan to hear more
of these?

Knock, knock.
Who's there?
Aileen.
Aileen who?
Aileen against the door because I'm so tired!

Knock, knock.
Who's there?
Mikey.
Mikey who?
Mikey is stuck!

Knock, knock.
Who's there?
Amanda.
Amanda who?
Amanda the bed!

Knock, knock.
Who's there?
Butter.
Butter who?
Butter bring an umbrella –
it looks like rain.

Knock, knock.
Who's there?
Emmet.
Emmet who?
Emmet your service!

Knock, knock.
Who's there?
Woody.
Woody who?
Woody come if we asked him?

Knock, knock.
Who's there?
Scott.
Scott who?
Scott to be the afternoon after.

Knock, knock.
Who's there?
House.
House who?
House ya doing?

Knock, knock.
Who's there?
Ken.
Ken who?
Ken I come in or do I have to climb through the window?

Knock, knock.
Who's there?
Marilyn.
Marilyn who?
Marilyn, she'll make you a good wife.

Knock, knock.
Who's there?
Czech.
Czech who?
Czech and see!

Knock, knock.
Who's there?
Wilfred.
Wilfred who?
Wilfred come if we ask nicely?

221

Knock, knock.
Who's there?
Sophia.
Sophia who?
Sophia nothing . . . fear is pointless!

Knock, knock.
Who's there?
Vincent.
Vincent who?
Vincent me here.

Knock, knock.
Who's there?
Toto.
Toto who?
Totally devoted to you.

Knock, knock.
Who's there?
Howl.
Howl who?
Howl I know when it's lunchtime?

Knock, knock.
Who's there?
Pudding.
Pudding who?
Pudding my best foot forward!

Knock, knock.
Who's there?
Mustard.
Mustard who?
Mustard left my coat in the car.

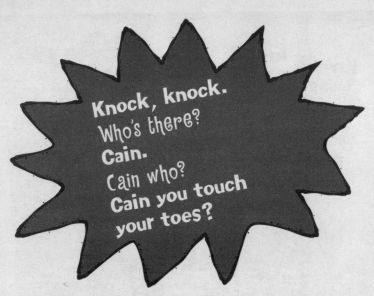

Knock, knock.
Who's there?
Cain.
Cain who?
Cain you touch
your toes?

Knock, knock.
Who's there?
Amazon.
Amazon who?
Amazon very good mood.

Knock, knock.
Who's there?
Watson.
Watson who?
Watson telly tonight?

Knock, knock.
Who's there?
Debbie.
Debbie who?
Debbie or not to be.

Knock, knock.
Who's there?
Turner.
Turner who?
Turner handle and open the door.

Knock, knock.
Who's there?
Ina Minnie.
Ina Minnie who?
Ina Minnie miney mo.

Knock, knock.
Who's there?
Red.
Red who?
Red any good books lately?

Knock, knock.
Who's there?
Hobbit.
Hobbit who?
Hobbit-forming.

Knock, knock.
Who's there?
Morrissey.
Morrissey who?
Morrissey the pretty birdies?

226

Knock, knock.
Who's there?
Thistle.
Thistle who?
Thistle have to do you until lunch is ready.

Knock, knock.
Who's there?
Disk.
Disk who?
Diskusting!

Knock, knock.
Who's there?
Misha.
Misha who?
Misha lots of things while you were away.

Knock, knock.
Who's there?
Gazza.
Gazza who?
Gazza kiss.

Knock, knock.
Who's there?
Aardvark.
Aardvark who?
Aardvark a million miles
to see you smile!

Knock, knock.
Who's there?
Police.
Police who?
Police stop telling these
awful knock-knock jokes!

Knock, knock.
Who's there?
Gorilla.
Gorilla who?
Gorilla me a steak – I'm starving!

Knock, knock.
Who's there?
Ketchup.
Ketchup who?
Ketchup to me and I'll tell you!

Knock, knock.
Who's there?
Cargo.
Cargo who?
Cargo vroom vroom.

Knock, knock.
Who's there?
Annie.
Annie who?
Annie thing you can do,
I can do better!

Knock, knock.
Who's there?
Armageddon.
Armageddon who?
Armageddon outta here!

Knock, knock.
Who's there?
Norma Lee.
Norma Lee who?
Norma Lee I can let myself in,
but I lost my key!

Knock, knock.
Who's there?
Hawaii.
Hawaii who?
I'm fine. Hawaii you?

Knock, knock.
Who's there?
Tad.
Tad who?
Tad's all folks!

DOCTOR, DOCTOR!

Is there a doctor in the house?

'Doctor, Doctor,
I keep on thinking I'm a moth!'
'Just get out of my light, will you?'

'Doctor, Doctor,
I keep thinking I'm a
wigwam and a tepee.'
'Calm down, you're two tents!'

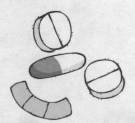

'Doctor, Doctor,
I keep thinking I'm a bee!'
'Oh, buzz off - can't you see I'm busy?'

'Doctor, Doctor, my hair keeps falling out. Can you give me something to keep it in?'
'Certainly! How about this paper bag?'

'Doctor, Doctor, I've only got fifty-seven seconds to live!'
'Wait a minute, will you?'

'Doctor, Doctor, my son just swallowed a pencil. What should I do?'
'Use a pen until I get there.'

233

'Doctor, Doctor, I've got lettuce stuck in the back of my throat!'
'By the looks of things, that's just the tip of the iceberg!'

'Doctor, Doctor, I think I might have magical powers!'
'Dear me, you had better lie down for a spell.'

'Doctor, Doctor, I keep on getting shooting pains in my eye when I drink tea!'
'Have you tried taking the spoon out?'

'Doctor, Doctor,
I keep on thinking
I'm a cat.'

'Take a seat, please.'

'I can't, I'm not
allowed to sit on
the furniture.'

'Doctor, Doctor,
I feel like a pack of cards.'

'I'll deal with you later.'

'Doctor, Doctor,
I've just swallowed a camera!'

'Don't worry, nothing serious will develop.'

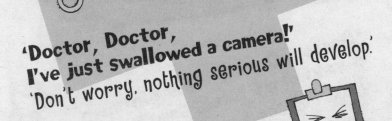

'Doctor, Doctor, it's been one month since my last visit and I still have this itchy rash!'
'Did you follow the instructions on the cream I gave you?'
'Yes, it says, "Keep lid tightly closed".'

'Doctor, Doctor, can you tell me how to live in the present?'
'yes, but not just now.'

'Doctor, Doctor, this ointment is making my hands smart.'
'Quick, rub some on your head!'

'Doctor, Doctor, all my daughter does is lie in bed and eat beeswax and yeast.'
'Don't worry, one day she'll rise and shine.'

'Doctor, Doctor, I keep on thinking I'm a snowman.'
'One day it will drift away.'

'Doctor, Doctor, I think I'm a shepherd.'
'Oh, I wouldn't lose any sheep over it.'

'Doctor, Doctor, I keep on thinking I'm a twenty-pound note.'

'I recommend you spend a week at the seaside - the change will do you good.'

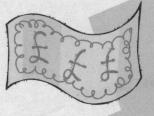

'Doctor, Doctor, everybody thinks I am a liar!'

'Come now — I find that hard to believe.'

'Doctor, Doctor, I keep on thinking I'm a pig.'

'Really, and how do you feel?'

'Swine, thanks!'

'Doctor, Doctor, you have to help me out!'
'Certainly – which way did you come in?'

'Doctor, Doctor, I feel like an apple!'
'We must get to the core of this!'

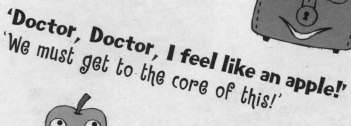

Doctor: 'I have some good news and some bad news.'

Patient: 'What's the bad news?'

Doctor: 'The bad news is that you have a horrible new fatal disease.'

Patient: 'Oh no! What's the good news?'

Doctor: 'The good news is that we name the disease after you and you will become terribly famous!'

'Doctor, Doctor,
I keep on
thinking I'm
a waste-paper
basket.'
'Don't talk
rubbish.'

'Doctor, Doctor,
I keep on forgetting things.'
'When did this start happening?'
'When did what start happening?'

'Doctor, Doctor, I still don't feel any better!'
'Did you take your medicine after the bath?'
'After drinking the bathwater, there wasn't any room for the medicine!'

'Doctor, Doctor, I can't sleep at night!'
'Sleep on top of the cupboard – you'll soon drop off.'

'Doctor, Doctor,
I feel like a pair of curtains.'
'Pull yourself together, man!'

'Doctor, Doctor,
I'm very windy!'
'Get yourself a kite, then!'

'What did the computer die of?'
'A terminal illness.'

THE WORST THINGS TO HEAR IN THE OPERATING THEATRE

'Somebody remind me,
what are we taking out today?'

'Shouldn't that machine be beeping?'

'Did anyone see where my
contact lens went?'

'The last time I performed this
operation was back in '76 . . .'

'Somebody get that dog out of here!'

'Is this rust or blood on this knife?'

'Doctor, Doctor, I feel like a clam!'
'Don't worry, we'll soon have
you out of your shell.'

'What did the doctor advise the train conductor to do with his food?'
'Chew, chew.'

'Doctor, Doctor, I keep on thinking there are monsters under my bed!'
'I see. Why don't you try sleeping on the floor?'

'Doctor, Doctor, I've just swallowed my mouth organ!'
'Thank goodness you weren't playing your piano.'

'Doctor, Doctor, my baby is the spitting image of me.'
'So long as she is healthy!'

'Doctor, Doctor, I keep on seeing double.'
'Lie down on the couch.'
'Which one?'

'Doctor, Doctor, I think I caught a bug. What should I do?'
'Let's open the window and let it out.'

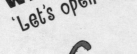

244

'Doctor, Doctor, I feel like a pin.'
'I see your point.'

'Doctor, Doctor, I feel like a power line.'
'How shocking!'

'Doctor, Doctor, everyone keeps on ignoring me!'
'Next, please!'

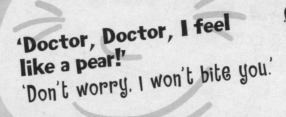

'Doctor, Doctor, I feel like a pear!'
'Don't worry. I won't bite you.'

'Doctor, Doctor, I feel like an elastic band!'
'You'll snap out of it soon enough.'

'Doctor, Doctor, I've got purple spots at the back of my throat.'
'Go to the office next door and stick out your tongue.'
'Will that help?'
'No, but I find the other doctor really annoying.'

'Doctor, Doctor, I feel like an octopus.'
'Oh, get a grip, man!'

'Doctor, Doctor, my husband has swallowed an extra-large bottle of aspirin.'
'Give him an extra-large headache.'

'Doctor, Doctor, a pumpkin seed went down the wrong way.'
'Don't worry, you'll be vine.'

'Doctor, Doctor, everyone thinks I'm really boring!'
'Just keep talking while I take a nap.'

'Doctor, Doctor – how can I stop my nose from running?'
'Simple – hide your nose's trainers!'

'Why did the old house go to the doctor's?'
'Because of its window panes.'

A nurse came into the operating theatre and found a doctor sticking a needle into an empty bed.

'How are you feeling, Doctor?' the nurse asked.

'Oh, I'm fine,' said the doctor. 'But this invisible man needs help.'

Why did the doctor operate on his book?
To take out the appendix.

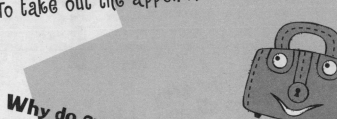

Why do surgeons make good comedians?
They always have people in stitches.

What did the doctor say to the tree?
'Your bark is worse than your blight.'

Why did the TV producer visit the doctor?
To have his cast removed.

What's big and grey with needles all over it?
An elephant undergoing acupuncture.

Why did the bee go to the doctor's?
Because it had hives.

What do you call a group outing for surgeons?
A doc-tour.

What is the best time to go to the dentist's?
Tooth hurty (Two thirty).

Why did the shark keep on getting holes in his teeth?
Because he ate so many jellyfish.

Why are dentists always so unhappy?
Because they're always looking down in the mouth.

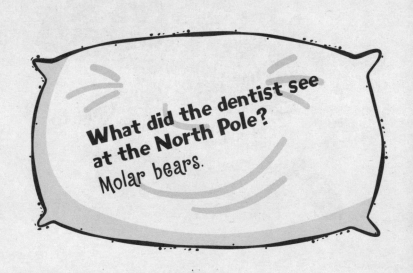

What did the dentist see at the North Pole?
Molar bears.

Why did the prince go to the dentist?
To get crowned.

What do you call an old dentist?
Long in the tooth.

Dentist: 'It'll only take a minute to take this bad tooth out.'

Patient: 'You have to take my tooth out? How much will it cost?'

Dentist: 'One hundred pounds.'

Patient: 'That much for a procedure that only takes a minute?'

Dentist: 'If you prefer, I could take it out very slowly.'

Did you hear about the judge who went to the dentist's? He asked her to extract the tooth, the whole tooth and nothing but the tooth.

How do Eskimos stop their mouths from freezing up?
They grit their teeth.

What is a dentist's favourite childhood game?
Caps and robbers.

What does a dentist do in a high-speed car chase?
He braces himself.

What did the polite vampire say to the dentist?
'Fangs very much.'

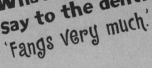

LUCKY DIP

Truly stupid jokes about anything and everything.

Why do clocks die?
Because their time is up.

Why did the bald man have no use for keys?
He didn't have any locks.

Why don't bananas like the sun?
They always peel.

What did the envelope say to the stamp?
'Stick with me, baby, and we'll go places!'

What did the dishcloth say to the worktop?
'I'm wiped out!'

What are microwaves?
Tiny greetings.

What did the saucer say to the cup?
'None of your lip!'

What invention allows people to see through walls?
Windows.

What did the tin say to the tin opener?
'You make me flip my lid!'

Do you know the time?
'No, we haven't met yet.'

What's the height of stupidity?
I don't know. How tall are you?

Why don't robots have brothers?
They all have trans-sisters.

A butcher is seven feet tall and wears size fourteen shoes. What does he weigh?
Sausages.

What goes woof tick, woof tick, woof tick?
A watch dog.

What two words have the most letters?
Post office.

Why did the truck go over the hill?
Because it couldn't go under it.

What did the broom say to the mop?
'People keep pushing us around.'

Why did the girl put lipstick on her forehead?
She was trying to make-up her mind.

What is the most loyal animal?
The leech. Once they find someone they like, they stick to them.

What are hippies for?
To keep your leggies up.

What did one crisp say to the other?
Fancy a dip?

What sort of shoes does a plumber hate?
Clogs.

The News Headlines You Didn't Read . . .

Dirty crooks steal soap

Bicycle salesman peddles bikes

Postman is given the sack

Sweetmaker is making a mint

Waiter tipped over the edge

Comb given to exchange students as a parting gift

Door knocker designer wins No Bell prize

Lifeguard at sales saves a lot

What do stuntmen do in their free time? Just stay home to crash.

What kangaroo can jump higher than a palm tree? All of them. Palm trees can't jump.

What's the definition of a caterpillar? A hairy worm.

What happened to the lady who stole some mascara?
She got fifty lashes.

What do you call an adult balloon?
A blown-up.

Which type of keys scratch themselves under their arms?
Monkeys!

What has fifty legs but can't walk?
A centipede.

Why didn't the bicycle go for a ride?
It was two tyred.

What is green, has four legs and if it fell out of a tree it would kill you?
A pool table.

'You have the brain of an idiot.'
'Do you want it back?'

Why was the broom late?
It overswept.

Why did the orange stop rolling?
It ran out of juice.

Two sheep were in a field.
'Baaaa!' said one.
'I was going to say that!'
said the other.

What's brown and sticky?
A stick.

Did Adam and Eve ever have a date?
No, just an apple.

What do you call a plate that isn't truthful?
Dish-honest.

How did the gravedigger get his job?
He just fell into it.

Why was the rubbish sad?
It was down in the dumps.

Have you ever seen a barn dance?
No, but I've seen a chimney sweep.

Why was the banker upset?
He lost interest in everything.

What always goes to bed with its shoes on?
A horse.

What do you serve but never eat?
A tennis ball.

Why did the human cannonball lose his job?
He got fired.

Why should Parisians always carry sunscreen on holiday?
Because French fry.

Why should you never wear polka dots when playing hide-and-seek?
You'll always be spotted.

What do you call an artificial stone?
A shamrock.

What animal cries a lot?
The whale.

What's the best way to break a bad habit?
To drop it.

What happened when someone trod on a grape?
It let out a little whine.

What's round, sad and lives in the boot of your car?
De-spair tyre.

How can you tell when an
orange is crazy?
When it's out of its rind.

What does a frog build
a house out of?
Rivets, rivets, rivets.

Where do
bow ties go
on holiday?
Thailand.

Why did Miss Muffet
need a road map?
She lost her whey.

What clothes do the
lawyers wear in court?
Lawsuits.

What do you call a boomerang
that doesn't come back?
A stick.

What do you call a dead grape?
A raisin.

What did the teacup say?
'I've been mugged.'

What's yellow and dangerous?
Shark-infested custard.

What happened when the king's men played a joke on Humpty Dumpty?
He fell for it.

What's the difference between a truck and an orange?
You can't pick up a truck.

Why won't you find aspirin in the jungle?
Because the parrots ate 'em all.

Why was the revolving door feeling blue?
Because everyone was always pushing it around.

What's big and yellow and eats rocks?
A big yellow rock-eater.

What is the difference between an Indian elephant and an African elephant?
About 3,000 miles.

Why are sausages rude?
Because they spit.

What's yellow and stupid?
Thick custard.

What's invisible and smells like a banana?
A monkey's fart.

What do you call a girl who stands astride a river?
Bridget.

Did you hear about the man who bought a paper shop?
It blew away.

What do hairdressers study?
Short cuts.

Why did the toilet paper
roll down the hill?
Because it wanted to
get to the bottom.

Who is the world's
first underwater spy?
James Pond.

'I bought a rug on eBay
in mint condition.'
'Oh, that's great.'
'Yes, it had a hole in
the middle.'

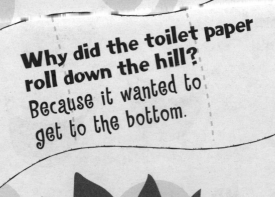

'I have five eyes, six ears and three mouths. What am I?'
'Quite ugly.'

What do you call a man with a rabbit up his jumper? Warren.

What do you call a man with a shovel on his head? Doug.

**What do you call a man
with a seagull on his head?**
Cliff.

'You remind me of the sea.'
'Why, because I'm so mysterious?'
'No – you make me feel sick.'

**What did the chimney sweep
say about his job?**
'It soots me.'

What part of the army can a baby work in?
The infantry.

How should you dress on a cold day?
Quickly.

What is a complete waste of time?
Telling a hair-raising story to a bald man.

What has keys but never opens a lock?
A piano.

What's the most shocking city in the world?
Electri-city.

What grows up while it grows down?
A baby penguin.

What pets make the most noise?
Trum-pets.

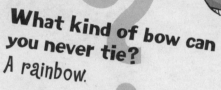

What kind of bow can you never tie?
A rainbow.

Why is the letter 'T' like an island?
They are both in the middle of water.

What begins with 'T'
ends in 'T' and has 'T' in it?
A teapot.

What grows bigger the
more you take from it?
A hole.

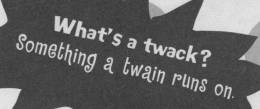

What's a twack?
Something a twain runs on.

Angry motorist: 'I'll teach you to throw stones at my new car!'

Boy: 'I wish you would. I've thrown about five stones and haven't hit it yet!'

What happens when a ball stops rolling?
It looks round.

Why is the letter 'E' lazy?
Because it's always in bed.

Why were the fleas playing football in a saucer?
Because they were playing for the cup.

What is small and purple and calls out for help?
A damson in distress.

What is long, wears a brown hat and lies in a box?
A match.

Why did the cookie cry?
Cos her mother had been a wafer so long.

What's yellow on the outside and green on the inside?
A cucumber dressed as a banana.

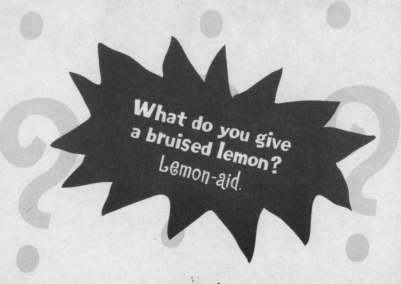

What do you give a bruised lemon?
Lemon-aid.

How does the moon cut his hair?
E-clipse it.

Why did the tomato blush?
Because it saw the salad dressing.

What vegetable should you serve with a jacket potato?
Button mushrooms.

Why did the orange tree cry?
Because people were always picking on him.

What letter is a vegetable?
A 'P'.

What did the picture say to the wall?
'I've got you covered.'

How do you make a cream puff?
Chase it round the garden.

How do you make a sausage roll?
Push it down a hill.

Two ears of corn ran
up a hill. What were
they when they got
to the top?
Puffed wheat.

Why didn't the teddy bear want
a second helping of dessert?
Because he was stuffed.

Where did the king
keep his armies?
Up his sleevies.

What do you call a man
who doesn't sink?
Bob.

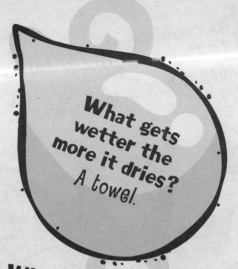

What gets wetter the more it dries?
A towel.

What did the stag say to his children?
'Let's go, deers.'

Mother: 'Poor Jane, did the bee sting you?'

Jane: 'Yes! (sobbing)'

Mother: 'Let's put some cream on it then.'

Jane: 'Don't be silly – it'll be miles away by now!'

295

Why couldn't the butterfly go to the dance?
Because it was a moth-ball.

What did the big candle say to the little candle?
'You're too young to go out.'

Did you hear about the hyena that ate a pack of Oxo cubes?
He made himself a laughing stock.

How do sheep keep warm in winter?
They turn on the central bleating.

What must you be
careful not to do when
it's raining cats and dogs?
Step in a poodle.

What do lazy dogs do for fun?
They chase parked cars.

'Anything good on the television tonight?'
'Just the same as usual. The goldfish bowl.'

What did the little light bulb say to his mum?
'I wuv you watts and watts.'

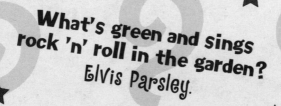

What's green and sings rock 'n' roll in the garden?
Elvis Parsley.

What is brown, prickly and squirts jam?
A hedgehog eating a doughnut.

What's round and bad-tempered?
A vicious circle.

What starts with 'E', ends in 'E' and has an 'E' in it?
An envelope.

Why do you go to bed?
Because the bed won't go to you!

Why did the tap run?
Cos it saw the kitchen sink.

What do you get if you dial 567534291 0768935271209108373739320283 729022838377238292O2?
A sore thumb.

What did one magnet say to the other magnet?
'You're very attractive.'

Why are parks dangerous?
Because of all the dande-lions.

What kind of biscuit do you find at the South Pole?
A penguin.

What has sixty feet and sings?
The school choir.

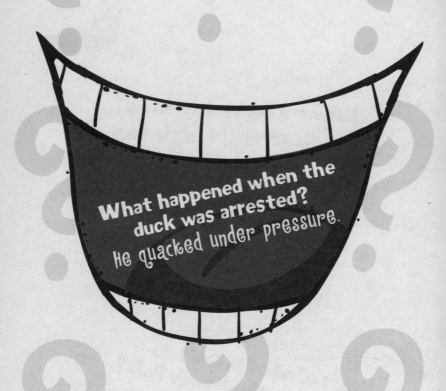

What happened when the duck was arrested?
He quacked under pressure.

What happens if you throw a white stone in the Red Sea?
It gets wet!

Why don't mountains get cold in the winter?
Because they wear snow caps.

Did you hear about the chef who got an electric shock?
He stood on a bun and a currant shot up his leg.

If two's company and three's a crowd, what are four and five?
Nine.

Why would Snow White make a great judge?
Because she's the fairest of them all.

What is full of holes yet can still hold water?
A sponge!

What keeps jazz musicians grounded?
Groovity.

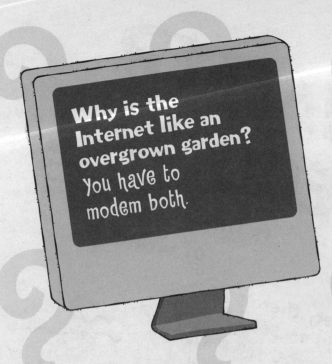

Why is the
Internet like an
overgrown garden?
You have to
modem both.

What can a lizard do that a snake can't?
Stretch its legs.

How many idiots does it take to make chocolate chip cookies?
20 – one to make the dough
and nineteen to peel the M&Ms.

WAITER SECOND...

Is this a whole bunch of waiter jokes?

'Waiter, there's a fly in my soup.'

'Don't worry, the spider in the salad will soon get it.'

'Waiter, what's this fly doing in my soup?'

'It looks like backstroke, sir.'

'Waiter, is there soup on the menu?'
'No, sir, I wiped it off.'

'Waiter, this chicken tastes funny.'
'Why aren't you laughing, then?'

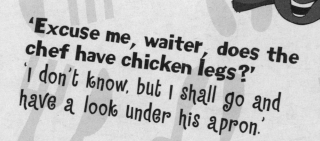

'Excuse me, waiter, does the chef have chicken legs?'
'I don't know, but I shall go and have a look under his apron.'

Waiter: 'I'm sorry, have you been waiting long?'
Customer: 'Did you know that you have 2,142 tiles on your ceiling?'

'**Waiter, how do you serve shrimp here?**'
'Just the usual way. On a plate.'

'**Waiter, this fish is bad!**'
'Oh dear, I am sorry. You naughty, naughty fish!'

'**Waiter, there's a fly in my soup.**'
'Just wait there, I'll call the RSPCA.'

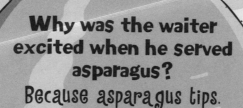

Why was the waiter
excited when he served
asparagus?
Because asparagus tips.

'Waiter, your thumb is in my soup!'
'Oh, I can assure you it isn't hot.'

Did you hear about the new
restaurant on the moon?
Great view but no atmosphere.

'**Waiter, there's a fly in my soup.**'
'Yes, it's the heat that kills them.'

'**Waiter, there's a cockroach in my soup.**'
'Well, it's the fly's day off.'

What did the frog say when it saw the fly in the soup?
'Is that all I get?'

'Waiter, what is this?'
'That's bean salad, sir.'
'I know what it's been, but what is it now?'

Waiter: 'And how did you find your steak, madam?'
Lady: 'I moved a lettuce leaf and there it was.'

'Waiter, there's a flea in my soup!'
'I'll tell him to hop it.'

'Waiter, do you serve crabs?'
'Sit down, sir, we serve anyone.'

'Waiter, is this all you have for dinner?'
'No, sir — I'll be having a nice roast when I get home.'

'Waiter, there's a twig on my plate.'
'Yes, we have branches everywhere.'

'Waiter, there's a hair in the honey!'
'It must have dropped off the comb.'

'Waiter, there's a contact
lens in my glass!'
'Why, thank you, I've been
looking for that everywhere.'

Man: 'I'll have some lamb chops,
please, and make them lean.'
Waiter: 'Certainly, sir – which way?'

'Waiter, why have you served my meal in a feedbag?'
'Your companion said you ate like a horse!'

'Waiter, why isn't there any chicken in my chicken pie?'
'You wouldn't expect to find a dog in a dog biscuit, would you?'

SPORTING MOMENTS

The expression 'sporting mad' certainly applies to this chapter – these jokes are nuts!

Did you hear about Pinocchio when he entered the 100-metre race?
He won by a nose-length.

How do you start a jelly race?
Say 'get set'.

What race is never run?
A swimming race.

What does a winner lose in a race?
Her breath.

What's a sprinter's favourite drink?
Running water.

What did one domino say to the other?
'Aren't you tired of being a pushover?'

Why did the football quit the team?
It was tired of being kicked around.

What do you say to a skiing elephant?
Don't say anything, just get out of the way!

How do you service a pogo stick?
By giving it a spring clean.

Did you hear about the blind grandfather who went sky-diving? He loved it, but his guide dog wasn't too happy about it.

Two greyhounds were in a kennel, boasting about their skills on the track.

'I've won seven of my last twenty races,' said the first one.

'That's nothing, I've won fifteen of my last twenty-two,' said the other.

A horse that was in a stall nearby poked his head out.

'Excuse me, that's really impressive, but I've won seventy-five of my seventy-six races.'

The greyhounds were amazed.

'Wow, did you see that?' said the first dog. 'A horse that can talk!'

Why are the floors of
basketball courts wet?
The players dribble a lot.

'**What's up, Richard?**'
'I've had bad news. My doctor
says I can't play rugby.'
'**Really? I didn't even
know he'd seen you play!**'

What team have never met
each other before?
Queen's Park Strangers.

Why don't elephants ride motorbikes?
Their ears won't fit in their helmets.

'Hey, coach, the doctor says I can't play football.'
'I could have told you that.'

Why did the tennis coach give his team a lighter?
Because they kept losing their matches.

Did you hear about the tennis player who went to jail?
He was charged with making a racket.

What type of footballer is best at lighting a match?
A striker.

What do footballers like to drink?
Penal-tea.

Why did a couple of young cows chase a ball round the football pitch?
It was a game of two calves.

Why should you never
put vampires in goal?
Because they don't like crosses.

If you have a
referee in football,
what do you
have in bowls?
Soup.

A cricket walked into a sports shop.
'Hello,' said the sales assistant.
'Do you know there is a
sport named after you?'
'**What?**' said the cricket, surprised.
'There is a game called Billy?'

Two boys were talking about cricket:
'The local team wants me to play for them badly.'
'Well, then, you are the right person
for the job.'

Why does Dracula love
cricket so much?
Because of all the bats.

An alien returned to his spaceship
from Earth and explained to his fellow
crew a strange ceremony he had just
observed:
'Surrounding a large green field were
several thousand worshippers. Two priests
faced each other along a strip and each
knocked three spears into the ground.
Eleven more priests walked out, clothed
all in white. Two high priests walked to the
centre, clutching clubs, and another priest
started to throw a red sphere at the
club-wielding priests.'
The aliens were amazed.
'What happened next?'
'It began to rain.'

Why did the footballers suddenly start to trip over?
They were playing injury time.

What do you say to a footballer with socks stuffed into his ears?
Anything you like – he can't hear you!

Why can't cars play rugby?
Because they only have one boot.

Did you hear about the rugby player who stayed up all night trying to figure out what happened when the sun went down?

It finally dawned on him.

What goes white and red, white and red?

An England rugby player rolling down a hill.

Jonny Wilkinson was watching TV one night when there was a knock at the door. When he opened it, there was a snail standing there.

'Get lost!' Jonny said, kicking the snail through the air.

One year later, Jonny was watching TV when there was another knock at the door. This time the same snail was there with a face like thunder.

Before Jonny could react, the snail shouted at him, 'What was that all about?'

Why did the footballer put a lump of sugar under his pillow every night?
So he could have sweet dreams.

What sort of trees do footballers have in their gardens?
Trans-firs.

What's the angriest part of a football pitch?
The crossbar.

Why aren't footballers artistic?
Because they don't like to draw.

Why didn't the football team go to the party?
It was a dive.

Why was the tennis court so chilly?
It was surrounded by fans.

Why didn't the dog play football?
Because it was a boxer.

When is a football player likely to come to your house?
When the door is open.

Why was Cinderella terrible at football?
Because she kept on running away from the ball.

Why was Cinderella terrible at football?
Have you ever tried kicking a ball in glass slippers?

Did you hear about the nun who wanted to be a footballer? She was trying to kick the habit.

A football player was walking a cheetah on a lead. 'Hey, where did you get him from?' a passer-by asked. 'I won him in a raffle,' said the cheetah.

A football fan called her cat Trouble. Late one evening after a big premiership match, the fan's cat didn't come home. Wearing her football strip, the fan took a baseball bat just in case she came cross anything nasty and combed the streets looking for her cat. A policeman spotted her. 'What are you up to, eh?' the policeman asked. 'Oh, don't worry. I'm just looking for Trouble,' the fan said.

Why do gymnasts like going to taverns across the road from each other?
They like parallel bars.

Why did the Olympian eat bits of metal?
It was his staple diet.

What is the fastest thing in the world?
Milk — it is pasteurized before you know it.

Did you hear about the swimmer who would only do the backstroke after lunch?
She didn't want to swim on a full stomach.

Why was the jockey so small?
He was raised on condensed milk.

'When I was rock climbing last year, I fell off a twenty-metre cliff.'
'Goodness. Were you hurt?'
'No, I had only gone up one metre.'

Why did the veteran climber refuse to scale Everest?
He was already over the hill.

How did the climber feel when he tumbled down the hill?
Crestfallen.

Why is a doughnut like a golfer?
It has a hole in one.

What do you call a person who does arithmetic and runs races? A mathlete.

A huge sumo wrestler ran into a jockey on the street. 'Dear me, you are small,' said the sumo wrestler. 'Yes, I know,' replied the jockey, 'but I haven't been very well lately.'

Hunter 1: 'I say, you've just shot my wife!'

Hunter 2: 'I'm terribly sorry, old chap. Here, take a shot at mine.'

How do chess players start bedtime stories?

'Once a-pawn a time . . .'

CHRISTMAS CORKERS

Have a cracking good time with these festive jokes!

What cars do Santa's elves prefer to drive?
Toy-otas.

One Christmas morning Luke Skywalker and his father, Darth Vader, are sitting round the tree. Vader hands Luke his first present and Luke says, without opening it,

'I know what this one is. It's a robot.'

Sure enough, he opens it and it is the latest model robot. Vader is very pleased and hands his son the second present.

'Oh great, Dad, it's a new light sabre.'

Luke opens his gift and it is a brand-new light sabre. Impressed, Vader hands him his third present and, before he gets the paper off, Luke says,

'Brilliant! A new robe!'

Vader is amazed and asks his son how he knew what they all were. Luke looks a bit sheepish and says,

'I felt the presents, Dad . . .'

What's a frog's favourite part of Christmas?
Mistletoad.

What do you call people who are afraid of Santa?
Claustrophobic.

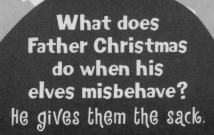

What does Father Christmas do when his elves misbehave?
He gives them the sack.

What does Santa feed his elves?
Fairy cakes.

What does Santa make his bread out of?
Elf-raising flour.

What nationality is Santa Claus?
North Polish.

Did you hear about the time the Tooth Fairy swapped places with Santa Claus?
On Christmas morning, every child found a pound under the Christmas tree and a bicycle under their pillow.

What do elves learn at school?
The elf-abet!

Why was Santa's little helper depressed?
He had little elf-esteem.

Christmas Wish List

A bank robber:
tights

An electrician:
shorts

A mummy:
a body wrap

A spider:
four pairs of socks

Lauren: 'I'm going to have a puppy for Christmas!'

Sophie: 'Really? We always have turkey!'

How do angels greet each other?
'Halo!'

What did the
big cracker say to
the little cracker?
'My pop is bigger
than yours!'

Eugene was given a lamp
for his birthday by his sister.
'It's a magic lamp,'
she told him excitedly.
'Rub it and see what happens.'
So Eugene rubbed the lamp and a
genie appeared. 'I will give you
three wishes,' the genie said.
'I want to be richer than the Queen,'
Eugene said. Suddenly, a huge mound
of treasure appeared beside him.
'I want to play football like Wayne Rooney,'
Eugene said, and whoosh, he was decked
out in a football kit.
'Finally,' Eugene said,
'I want to be irresistible to girls.'
In a puff of smoke, Eugene was turned
into a doll.

'Gran, will the mince pies be long?'
'No, don't be silly – they'll be round!'

Why can only two elves
fit under a toadstool?
Cos there isn't mushroom.

What are brown and
creep around the house?
Mince spies.

What is an adult's favourite
Christmas carol?
Silent Night.

What ailment is common
around Christmas?
Tinsel-itus!

Which candle burns longer –
a red one or a green one?
Neither – candles always burn shorter!

Who delivers your cat's Christmas presents?
Santa Paws.

Who delivers the presents to baby sharks?
Santa Jaws.

What bird has wings but cannot fly?
Roast turkey.

Why did the farmer try to mate a turkey with an octopus?
So at Christmas the whole family could have a leg each.

How does good King Wenceslas like his pizzas?
Deep and crisp and even.

What do you get in December that you don't get any other month?
The letter 'D'.

What did Adam say the night before Christmas?
'It's Christmas, Eve.'

What's the difference between the alphabet and the Christmas alphabet?
The Christmas alphabet has No 'L'.

What do ghosts put on their Christmas turkey?
Grave-y.

Top Nine Things to do with Leftover Turkey

1. **Make turkey casserole**
2. **Make turkey curry**
3. **Make turkey stir-fry**
4. **Make a turkey pie**
5. **Make a turkey layer cake**
6. **Make your friends feel sick by offering any of the above when they come round**
7. **Throw bits at the next-door neighbours' cat**
8. **Make a turkey bonfire**
9. **Throw it in the bin**

Why did the boy eat all the leftover turkey?
Because he was a turkey gobbler!

Where do Christmas turkeys go when they die?
To oven.

Why are Christmas trees so terrible at sewing?
They drop their needles everywhere.

What did one snowman say to the other?
'Ice to see you.'

How do you know if a snowman has been sleeping in your bed?
You wake up wet.

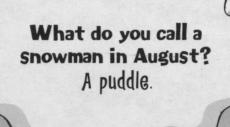

**What do you call a
snowman in August?**
A puddle.

**What do you say to a
stressed-out snowman?**
'Chill out!'

How do snowmen prefer to travel?
By ice-icle.

What kind of adhesivo do they use in the North Pole?

I-gloo.

My brother makes sure he puts his sock out for Santa every year. He doesn't need to hang it –

it stands up all by itself.

What do you get if you cross a Christmas tree with an apple?

A pineapple.

Who's impossible to overtake at Christmas?
The three wide men!

What did the father snowman say to his son when they got inside the igloo?
'Don't turn on the heater!'

Knock, knock.
Who's there?
Mary.
Mary who?
Mary Christmas!

Knock, knock.
Who's there?
Wenceslas.
Wenceslas who?
Wenceslas bus home?

Knock, knock.
Who's there?
Wayne.
Wayne who?
Wayne in a manger.

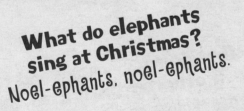

What do elephants sing at Christmas?
Noel-ephants, noel-ephants.

353

Why did the elf want to
get the Internet?
So he could build a gnome page.

'Why is this Christmas
cake so crunchy?'
'Try spitting out the plate.'

What do angry mice send to
each other at Christmas time?
Cross-mouse cards.

What is the wettest animal?
The rain-deer.

What do reindeer have that no other animal has?
Baby reindeer.

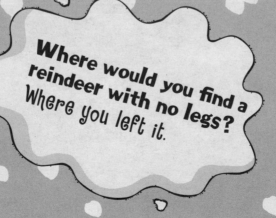

Where would you find a reindeer with no legs?
Where you left it.

Why did the reindeer wear sunglasses at the beach?
Cos he didn't want to be recognized!

What do you call a deer with no eyes?
No eye deer.

Where does mistletoe go to become famous?
Hollywood!

What's the most popular wine at Christmas?
'I don't like sprouts!'

What does Santa suffer from if he gets stuck in a chimney?
Claus-trophobia.

EASTER MIRTH

This collection is truly eggs-cellent!

Is it true eating lots of carrots helps your eyesight?
Well, you never see the Easter bunny in glasses, do you?

Why is the bunny the luckiest animal in the world?
Because he has four rabbit's feet.

Why does the Easter bunny have such a shiny nose?
His powder puff is on the other end.

What do you get if you pour hot water down a rabbit hole?
A hot cross bunny.

What do you get if you cross the Easter bunny with a parrot?
A rabbit that will tell you where it laid its eggs.

What do you call a bunny with a large head?
Egg-head!

How do you make a rabbit stew?
Keep it waiting for a few hours.

Why was the Easter bunny sad?
Because it was having a bad hare-day!

Why shouldn't you tell an Easter egg a joke?
It might crack up.

What did one Easter egg say to the other?
'Got any good yolks?'

What do you call a rabbit that tells good jokes?
A funny bunny.

How do you catch an Easter bunny?
Act like a carrot.

What side of a rabbit has the most fur?
The outside.

Why do bunnies like Easter eggs?
Cos they think they are eggs-cellent.

'I like your Easter tie.'
'Thanks. But why do you call it my Easter tie?'
'Because it's got egg all over it